KHACHE PHALU'S ADVICE ON THE ART OF LIVING

(Kha-che Pha-lu'i rNamthar)

KHACHE PHALU'S ADVICE ON THE ART OF LIVING

(Kha-che Pha-lu'i rNamthar)

Translated by
DAWA NORBU

LIBRARY OF TIBETAN WORKS & ARCHIVES

ISBN: 81-85102-64-3
Cover Art: Dr. Dawa

Published by the Library of Tibetan Works and Archives,
Dharamsala and printed at Indraprastha Press (CBT),
4, Bahadur Shah Zafar Marg, New Delhi 110002, India

In loving memory of my mother (1915-1985)
whose advice reminds me of
Khache Phalu's

Contents

Publisher's Note

The 18th century Khache Phalu's Advice (**Kha-che Pha-lu'i rNam thar**) on the art of living has been very popular in Tibet; even to this day it is cited and readwith much fervor among the Tibetans.

For the first time it has been translated into English by Dr. Dawa Norbu, a young Tibetan scholar who has created a niche for himself in the world of Tibetan scholarship. While simplifying the poetic work he has endeavored to preserve the original flavor. Dr. Dawa Norbu is an Associate Professor of Central Asian Studies, Jawaharlal Nehru University, New Delhi.

By publishing this work, it is hoped that the inimitable Khache Phalu's wisdom will stimulate the benign tendencies in human nature and society, and will, in its own way, be efficacious in making human beings wiser, better, and happier.

Gyatsho Tshering
Director, LTWA.

August, 1987.

Acknowledgment

While translating this Tibetan text into English, the pleasant memories of all those who taught me Tibetan came to my mind, and I would like to thank them in a chronological order. First and foremost I record my gratitude to my late Mother for her foresight and concern in sending me to Tibetan schools at an early age; and to all those who taught me Tibetan: Kungo Loten, Gen Kunga Topla and Kungo Lawon in Sakya. Tibet; Geshe Lobsang Tharchin, Norbu chophel and Dumkhang Phuntsog Namgyal at the Tibetan Refugee School, Darjeeling; and Kungo Shakjang and Lungsher Chang-chub Dorji at Dr Graham's Homes, Kalimpong, India. More immediate help in various ways came from my brother Kesang Tenzin and Pempa Tsering. To all of these teachers and friends I extend my grateful thanks.

The Translator's Introduction

Tibetan has been so much associated with Buddhism that it appears strange to the common reader that a Muslim should write a well known treatise in that language. Actually, Khache Phalu is not the only Muslim who wrote in Tibetan; Tibetan in its archaic form is the mother-tongue for Muslims in Ladakh and Baltistan. Besides, in Tibet itself before 1959 there used to be about 3000 Muslim merchants settled in Lhasa, Tsethang and Shigatse.[1]

It is perhaps because of this apparent abnormality that the authorship of **Khache Phalu's Namthar (rnam-thar)** is very much disputed. On the one hand there is a popular belief among Tibetans that it was secretly written by a high lama who used the pen-name of Khache Phalu; a few presumed "experts" even name the VI Dalai Lama as the "real" author. On the other hand, Tibetan Muslims now living in exile fervently claim that it was written by one of their kin. The textual evidence, as we shall see, seems to support the latter claim.

"Khache" is the ancient Tibetan name for Kashmir when it was flourishing Buddhist country; with the arrival of Islam and subsequent conversion of the area of Islamic faith, "Khache" became, in the course of popular usage, synonymous with Islam. However, in Tibet there used to be two types of Muslim merchants, ones coming from Kashmir and other from China. As the name indicates, Khache Phalu came from Indian ancestry. The second name (Phalu) is more confusing; all the Tibetan Muslim interviewees emphasized that it should correctly be Fazur-alla instead of the highly Tibetanized "Phalu". It was probably a transcription difficulty or Tibetan corruption. A Muslim family who claimed Khache Phalu as coming from their ancestry showed me an old manuscript in Arabic and Tibetan. There his name was signed in Tibetan as Khache Phalug's Zui,[2] and in another place simply Khache Phalu' Zui. Thus, the name Fazuralla is not too far off.

However, we will continue to call him the name familiar to us in the history of Tibetan literature. Khache-Phalu was well-versed in Arabic, Persian and Urdu, and learned just enough Tibetan to carry on his business, as was the practice among the Tibetan Muslims. His rnam-thar, which actually belongs to the Legs-bshed genre, was based on three Persian classics that were then taught in Mosque schools in Tibet: **Gulistan, Bostan** and **Pantanama**.[3] But a close study indicates that **Khache Phalu's Namthar** is not an imitation of Persian classics, neither in its style nor in its content. It is in a class by itself. To be sure it is not the classic written by a highly educated lama or aristocrat who are the usual authors of the "Great Tradition". **Khache Phalu's Namthar** belongs to the "little tradition", and it is precisely in this that its unique position in the history of Tibetan literature resides. Since the little tradition had invariably been an oral process hardly ever committed to writing, **Khache Phalu's Namthar** is one of the very few, if not the only, written document belonging to the little tradition. Its value to social scientists therefore is immense. It opens an enormous vista to the folk-mind; its strength and weakness; its wisdom and follies; its suffering and yearning; its ideals and illusions; its social ethos and trickiness; in short, its way of life and world view. Never before have we had so much common sense with so little allusion to the classical literature. Never before have we had such a good glimpse into the workings of the folk-mind in Tibet.

As a merchant, Khache Phalu was strategically situated in Tibetan society. As a naturalized Tibetan, he was a participant, but as a Muslim, he was an observer. And above all, as a merchant, he came to observe all sections of Tibetan society. This is what makes this work so weighty and earthy. The incredible way in which he opens his work enables us to appreciate how well he understood the Tibetan faith in Buddhism and in particular his familiarity with the Buddhist stereotyped images of Holy India. He depicts India, not Mecca, as the paradise or heaven at which his readers are told to strive. This image, as we know, perfectly fits in the typical Buddhist vision of India as **Arya Bhumi** par excellence. The introduction is enough to trick the readers into believing that the author must be a pious Buddhist writing a legs-bshed. And indeed the fact that a Muslim's work is claimed by Tibetan Buddhists as theirs is indicative of the success with which Khache Phalu is able to depict the Tibetan mind in its essential mood.

But that he is a Muslim in a fundamental sense seems beyond doubt, and this is perhaps what makes his work unique as an Islamic interlude in Buddhist Tibet. Despite his liberal outlook, he firmly adheres to the Islamic dogma of monotheism throughout the text. At the beginning of his work, he invokes, like a lamaist author, his muse, but in his own terms; "I prostrate before the Chief of all Chiefs. In Tibetan he is called Godhar." Again while advising children to be grateful to their parents, the Khache declares, "Above is Godhar and below Him are the two parents." And in all sorts of difficulties, he urges his readers to rely on Allah's ultimate help.

While he sticks to the Islamic dogma as an article of faith, in essence he emerges as a cultural synthesizer. It is this second aspect of **Khache Phalu's Namthar** which should interest the student of comparative religion. The whole work is a testimony to the astonishing degree to which the Muslims in Tibet achieved a working spiritual consensus with the Tibetan Buddhist society. As a result, there was no case of Buddhist-Muslim conflict in Tibet.

What are the areas then in which such spiritual consensus seems evident in the rnamthar? The author appreciates the Tibetan philosophical view of life as a continuum to be lived here and hereafter, and not a problem to be solved. It reflects the human dilemma as symbolized by the unwillingness to give up either this or the next life. As he writes, "The purpose of this life and next is simultaneously achieved. This is in accordance with Khache Phalu's ink and pen." Again advising children to serve their parents, he cautions, "If your parents are not satisfied, both this and the next life are in vain." With respect to **Karma** with which the whole texture of his work is woven, the author bemoans: "There are many who utter **Karma** but practitioners of **Karma** are as scarce as gold." In fact in the first chapter, he outlines his themes as "the law of karma, sense of shame, love and compassion, custom and tradition etc.," all of which are Tibetan preoccupations.[4]

Indeed, apart from the few occasional Islamic dogmas such as the insistence upon monotheism and his class preoccupation with cost-and-gain mercantilism, the whole work may be considered as a fairly objective presentation of the Tibetan folk view of life and the universe in which it was lived.

Since he wrote it five or six generations ago in Shigatse at the time of Panchen Palden Yeshi (1738-1780) no blockprint of **Khache Phalu's Namthar** was ever made in Tibet; the author's handwritten manuscript was passed around from hand to hand until it became one of the most popular legs-bshed, perhaps next only to **Sakya Legs-bshed.** Its popularity may be gauged from the fact that the XII Dalai Lama censored the text, omitting such lines as those that directly exhort to Islamic faith and practice.[5] Some of its cryptic lines have indeed become part and parcel of common Tibetan expression.

The text on which the present tradition is based is one published by the Tibetan Cutural Printing Press in 1980. But this is the first translation ever untertaken.

Being never block-printed in Tibet, it is difficult to say what errors might have crept into the text. We don't know for example, what this line means; "Zoms-rtsa sten-la rgyag-thog med." Unlike lamaist works of similar genre, **Khache-Phalu's Namthar** is neither polished in its form nor systematic in its approach. Herein lies its anthropo-logical value- -getting the raw stuff as it is out of the horse's mouth. But it has also a natural beauty of its own closely akin to the common speech in Tibet. Its directness is indicative of the Tibetan character. The author never minces his words; he says simply and directly what he wants to say. His folksy wisdom is shot through earthy Tibetan imagery borrowed from everyday life in rural Tibet.

In keeping with his folksy style, I have adopted a "meaningful translation" (don-bsgyur) approach rather than a "a word for word" translation" (tsig-bsgyur). Translating a poetic work into another language with a different poetic sensibility poses a special problem; it pre-supposes that we know not only the two relevant languages but also two relevant cultures into which the translator must be well immersed. We have endeavored to render Tibetan poetry into its poetic equivalent in English, making sure that no meaning is lost in the process. Hence, we have again taken liberty to break one Tibetan line into two or more English lines in order to 'retain' the natural rhythm and directness of the original text. Thus, wherever possible, we have tried to convey not only the Tibetan meaning but its rhythm and music, without however violating the idiom or grammar of English language.

If it is devoid of much literary value in the "classical sense," where does the value of this unusual work lie? It resides as we have indicated earlier in two spheres: firstly as an anthropological world view of the Tibetan people; secondly as an Islamic interlude in Buddhist Tibet. On both accounts, it is a mine of ethnographic data for social scientists interested in Tibetan religion and society.

There is advice for us on a broad range of subjects: religion, death, inequality, contentment, education and the upbringing of children to name a few. If a philosophical summary of **Khache Phalu's Namthar** is at all possible, it may be this: That the ruler should rule his domain lawfully, that parents should bring up their children strictly, that everybody in society should know his limits and live according to the law of **Karma**.

Dawa Norbu
JNU, New Delhi
November, 1987

CHAPTER 1

Introductory

OM SVASTI! If I were to write and tell you all about the countless miracles and brilliant deeds that the Buddha, from the age of ten onwards performed in the Aryan land of India, and how auspicious signs and good omens in the world and particularly in the beloved neighboring areas occurred, this life-time and many more would be necessary to complete it.

Hence to tell you briefly
what the Buddha did
When he was ten years old;
he taught the following:
First, the treasure of truth;
second, how law came into being;
third, the ocean of shame;[1]
fourth, the ocean of charity;
fifth, his teachings based on the root-authority
whose tree grew up and whose branches multiplied.

      ***   ***   ***

Khache Phalu's written advice may be
a drop in the ocean of human culture-
law of karma, sense of shame (and respect),
love and compassion, custom and tradition etc.
This pearl of advice, hung in a string of verses,
is like a small stream of realization.

1

CHAPTER 2

Religion

The source of Dharma is the Vajra Throne;
behind is the Rocky Mountain of Dharma--high in its
  glory;
in front is the sea of compassion--full with glimmering
  light;
there summer or winter, day or night, is the same
  duration;
Summer is not hot, nor winter cold;
in such a place with perfect weather,
when the sun is right in the middle,
neither darkness nor shadows in the house.
These are the signs of the centre of the universe.
To go from such a place to an even better one,
I prostrate before the Chief of all chiefs!
In Tibetan He is "the most Precious One"[2]
And in our language "Godhar"![3]
If you want to go to the land of Aryans, India,
you must eliminate ignorance from your mind;
sink the black passions of desire and attachment
    to the bottom of the ocean;
(you must) burn out your greed and envy;
(you must) think, meditate and remember only one.[4]
If you think one is not dependent upon the other,
then my son, you must prepare of Dharma.
As you journey, you will see.....
What ever you do, will be religious;
whatever you send, will be in the right direction;
whatever you wish and desire, you will get in your
  hand;

whatever you say, will be well-said.
And whenever you bait, you will get the right number.
If you want to go to such a place,
you must have three essential qualities.
First, your mind should be as clean and as clear as a
      mirror;
second, your commitment should be as pure as the the
      River Tsangpo;
third, your courage should be like that of a lion.
If those three qualities are present,
then you have reached that place.
In order to reach such a place, young man,
you must be able to think for yourself;
otherwise, you might get stuck in this world.
Do not postpone it (religion) till tomorrow or day after
      tomorrow;
If you delay your practine, the caller (viz death) will
      come any day;
and then you will come to regret.

      ***   ***   ***

You can plant a Khasu[6] sapling upon a dry stone;
branches will instantaneously multiply,
and each branch will bear a name;
thus the intelligence of the learned
might not be lost.

      ***   ***   ***

The letter of request to the chief
must be presented to the chief himself.
If you forge the principal's letter and seal,
or the essence of the Chief's word,
you will be a sinful creature
like others in the world.

      ***   ***   ***

As a safe guard on the path of Dharma,
as someone of depend upon in this and the next life,
as someone to confide in and trust upon,
may I never separate from such a being!
May you see all this with your third eye
and keep it in your mind.
With your compassion and love, show the way.
May the big moon shine in the direction of Ling,
where smaller stars one thousand
and fifty two in number exist.
Have you understood what I have written?
Black writing is full of white meanings.
Whatever (I) Khache Phalu realized
and remembered—is offer

CHAPTER 3

Death

Religion and mundane reality are separate,
like mind and body are separate;
although mind wishes to die through penance,
body desires good food and to live happily.
But physical happiness might last only for three days,
whereas mental unhappiness looms large in the future.
If you want happiness,
your body must be prepared for penance,
and if you desire for physical pleasure,
your mind must be exposed to hardship.
If you listen to me,
you must keep your body and mind separate.

    ***   ***   ***

Once who exchanges gold for bronze is foolish.
If you mistake turquoise for a fake,
you must be stupid.
If you don't understand
the value difference between this life and the next,
you will waste this life time.
Not one or two years,
but even after a hundred years.
The elements of your body
will disappear in the soil.
As far as death is concerned,
there is no difference
between a king and a beggar in the street;
both will die.
The taste of good lasts

only while chewing;
life's joy and misery
last only for three days.
So even a beggar can go along with life;
a king might be happy
but will eventually die too.
How many died in the past,
we don't know;
how many will die in the future,
who can estimate?
People come and go.
In essence, whoever comes into being,
also will depart.
There is no certainty or
permanence in this life.
Where there is no certainty,
who knows the truth?
This uncertain and impermanent life is
like the setting sun beyond the hill;
it has to go; it can never stay there.

***   ***   ***

Still children should not waste their time;
if you are wise, you will concentrate on the essential,
and if you can do that,
you are the biggest hero.
Work in this life otherwise has no essence.
This world is not a permanent home;
it is like a travel lodge.
It is better to make one's own plans.
If a traveller does not prepare
in advance for the journey,
he cannot carry the lodge on his back;
nor can he take the hostess with him.

Think while the matter is in your hands;
when you have lost the key to the lodge,
it is a matter of regret.

***   ***   ***

Many might have lost their parents,
just as many children have survived.
But after the mother's death.
children are not likely to follow
(immediately).
Each one spends his allotted time and dies.
Each one must think for himself.
Preparation for your lonely journey
Must be done in advance
by giving charity to the poor.
You must teach your horse to trot
and be ready to leave the world.
If you want to be rich in the next life,
better think of the poverty of beggars now.
If you want to eat apricots later,
you must plant an apricot tree now;
you must plant roots for the benefit of all.

***   ***   ***

The basic practice of religion is
to keep a humanitarian attitude.
The essence of religion is to benefit others;
If you are merely interested in fulfilling your desires,
there is nothing better than alcoholic drinks.
The ego says, "I am, I am;"
it declares "I want money and reputation;"
"I want good food to eat and good clothes to wear;"
"I am the good and the handsome."
(If such a man goes on pilgrimage),
or meditates, his effort is in vain.

Even if he could live on the essence
of wind by meditation,
it is useless.
Such an advanced meditation is self-torture;
instead, cultured and elderly fathers are
better than a hundred selfish monks.
Selfish people have no sense of shame;
and those without shame are like animals.

***   ***   ***

Although a certain girl is distinguished
by ornaments and fine clothes,
that alone might not qualify her
for a respectable and wealthy man's wife.
Even if they engage in some religious practice
without concentration,
it will not be reflected in the mirror of purity.
The eye of the bull turning around a flour mill
is blinded by the curtain.
It may move round the whole day,
yet in the evening it finds itself
in the same spot.
If you cannot untie
the lasso of desire completely,
even the so called
best religious practice is empty.
If its wings are tied with a string,
even a vulture cannot fly.

***   ***   ***

You must have commitment
and perseverance from the heart.
Everything depends on your mind.
This path is meant
for those whose mind is alert.

You must cleanse your mind
again and again.
All must watch out
what others expect
what good name you have to bring
what good tradition you have to leave behind.
If all these three are present,
It is first among the first class.
This is Khache Phalu's heartfelt advice.
Whether to listen or not
is up to you,
but I have already written my ideas,
and my pen has exhausted them.

CHAPTER 4

Relations

The sun and moon, like umbrellas,
are the sky's ornaments;
they turn darkness into light
and fill the universe with this light.

Carnations are the gardens's ornaments;
when they blossom and glow
the garden is at its best.
A great king is the country's ornament.
If he is an accord with law,
his realm will be glorious and powerful.
If he is able to enforce law,
all his wishes will be fulfilled.
If his rule is an accord with law,
all will be happy and prosperous.

***   ***   ***

If the sea shakes,
fish will be naturally shaken.
If a country becomes poor,
the king will become naturally poor.
If aristocracy is flourishing,
it is due to the king's land.
If there were no subjects,
no feudal lord could exist.
Without the subjects
aristocracy will decline.
If aristocracy and subjects are ill at ease
then it is like a doctor who is sick.
Blood-letting[6] wounds
must be combined.

First, the deviant's case
must be considered carefully.
Second, if proved guilty,
he may be punished by whipping;
Third, evil criminals can be
done away with (i.e. put to death)
You cannot have compassion
for such criminals.

       ***   ***   ***

Before the lamb is taken away,
you must catch the wolf.
Before social disturbance sets in,
You must banish the culprits.
If the king sleeps till late,
he will not know till
society bleeds in conflict.
If the shepherd is intoxicated
with tea and bee,
the wolf will surely take away the sheep.
Whoever is the expert,
entrust the task to him;
a man who excels in carpentry
can't excel in painting.
A wolf may be good
but the shepherd cannot trust him.
Whoever believes in the law of karma,
appoint him as authority.
Make sure that the wolf
does not eat up the sheep.

       ***   ***   ***

The educated person concentrates
upon the essential.
If you want precious jewels,
they are at the bottom of the sea.

11

Trust those who follow their commitments.
You cannot mistrust a rock-like Vajra.
Day and night, consult the expert;
for even dead dogs in a salty lake
turn into salt.
With those who are affectionate,
cultivate good steady relations.
Those who reciprocate
have no regrets later.
Do not let down those
who have done things for you.
When you are able to do.
things for others,
here will be many others
who will do things for you.
With those who trust you,
have lasting relations.
Then good words about you
will resound through the world.
With the courageous, start good relations
before it is too late;
there might be an emergency
when you need his help.
When you fill your treasury with wealth,
make sure no enemy is left to steal.
There are two reasons why
you must subdue your enemies.
Enemies are out to steal your wealth;
without wealth, you don't attract
supporters either.
To seek supporters
you must have wealth.
If you have these two things,
enemies will naturally abound.

Use your wealth to help
your parents and children.
Listen to the advice of the aged one;
he has many experiences
of happiness and suffering to his credit.
When you reach the iron hill,
it's better to have the elderly's experience
than the youth's strength.

***   ***   ***

If you wish to defeat
your enemy at once,
first it's better
to be friendly and wait.
If you wish to achieve
your goal by strategy,
then to use bow and arrows,
swords and spears,
is a foolish way.
If you can't defeat your enemy,
better not fight him at all,
or why make many enemies.
Leave aside Denma[7];
even if you were Gesar,
it would be better to resolve problems
peacefully if possible.
Avoid any hero-like confrontation.

If it is a strategic shot,
shoot from a distance.
But first try ninety-nine
peaceful tactics,
and if your tactic fails
by the hundredth,

there is no alternative but to fight.

     ***   ***   ***

A man without imagination
is worse than a dog.
If it is a bad dog,
hit him with a stick on the nose.
it wants to go.
let it go on its way;
if it wants to fight,
let it walk three steps first.

When you don't remember
your anger at times
and if you recall later,
slap your own mouth.
If you want to achieve
your goals peacefully,
anger is useless.
If anger you conquered,
it's a sign of your education:
for one who follows his anger
is a stupid man.
If you can think ahead,
you are an intelligent man;
anyone can see the immediate cause
on the spot.
Anyone can see the white conch[8] broken.
Once broken it is difficult to mend;
so if your enemy approaches you
get rid of your anger.

     ***   ***   ***

But be careful of deceitful tricks.
A river may flow in the middle,

but without dams,
it overflows.
To befriend the evil man
is to hit the king.
To look after a thief's son
is to kill the merchant.
If you leave a poisonous snake alive,
it will harm people.
If you leave a wolf alive,
it will harm sheep.
Of course, dogs bite men,
and those who can
behead the evil persons,
and befriend the good people.

     ***   ***   ***

If you are too lenient towards the enemy,
he will be spoiled;
if you are too rough towards him,
he may take revenge later.
Mix both lenient and rough punishments.
Plan good strategy to deal
with both friends and enemies.

     ***   ***   ***

If you want to hold power,
sit on your golden throne impartially;
think of the well-being
of your kingdom and subjects.
At night (get off the throne and)
try hard religious practice;
pray with your body,
speech and mind.
For ultimate help,
rely on the 'Three Precious Jewels;''

act in accordance with the holy command.
If you want to have reputation
here and hereafter,
always remember death.
I, Khache Phalu, have
discussed and discussed,
and presented the essence
like pearls on a string
one by one
right in front of you.
When estimated,
the necklace costs hundreds.

CHAPTER 5

Contentment

In society there is too much inequality;
some are rich and some are poor;
as you can see there is no equality;
contentment is the best treatment for this.
What fate has decided, we can't alter.
It's better to follow the patterns of fate.
It is too bad even if one is
a donkey from Chang-rang;[9]
it has to carry its load.

      ***   ***   ***

Amount of wealth makes no difference
if one has the correct attitude.
Without contentment a king is a beggar;
with contentment a beggar is better off than the
king;
a king may be still hungry
living off his kingdom;
A beggar with a full bowl is contented and
proud.
if you are not contented
with what fate has decided,
then you are looking for suffering.
If you are contented,
wealth does not make a difference.
If fate so decides,
the enemy's wealth may be yours.
If fate has not so decided,
it might be difficult for a son
to inherit his father's wealth.

No vegetation grows on a stone,
and no amount of angry or
arrogant acting benefits.

        ***   ***   ***

If you want to fall in love,
go after a good father's son or daughter.
With contentment rest your
body and mind in peace.
Avoid all bad practices;
think of your father's peace
and son's happiness;
your reputation in this and
next is in your hand.
Khache Phalu's heartfelt advice overflows.
My spiritual sons, listen with your heart.
If you have intellegence,
I have written my lines.
Though not many,
what I delivered is delicious.

CHAPTER 6

Secrets

In summer look after metallic things
and in winter after your pottery.[10]
Both in summer and winter
watch your tongue.
Watch what secrets to tell
even your close friends.
For many are the friend-turned-enemies.

           ***   ***   ***

If necessary, you can ask others
to keep safe your valuables;
even if the keeper is gone,
you may find your valuables.
But if you ask others to keep your secrets,
you may live to regret.
Keep your innermost secrets
in the bottom of your heart,
and shut your mouth.
If the top secret leaks out,
it might cost even a man's life.
Then no amount of regret will help.
If you talk too much,
you might live to repeat
"Don't tell others as I used to."
If you don't watch your tongue,
your head might suffer later.
There is always a time
for the untold story,
but having regrets after telling a secret
is bad.

Before having told a secret
you have freedom.
Even if you told the truth of the matter,
there is the danger of others
maligning your truth.
A kindly advice may turn
into an unkindly act
in the enemy's hands.
Instead, be friendly to all,
friend or foe.

***   ***   ***

A wise man subdues
the evil intentions of a bad man.
One who is honest is on the religious path.
This is a happy state to be in,
for now and forever.
The purpose of this life and the next
is simultaneously
achieved.
This is in accordance with
Khache Phalu's ink and pen.
This is from the black letters
on the white paper.
The writer may be under the ground,
but what is written remains above.
Some men might discover it,
and it may remind them of
this secret advice.

CHAPTER 7

Human Nature

This world is like a mirror
into which we all look at each other.
Human existence is like an echo;
we keep answering each other.
Where you looked is reflected in the mirror;
What you have said
is echoed back by the hills.
A kindly deed is repaid
with a kindly deed.
An unkindly deed is repaid
with an unkindly deed.
This is how the cycle of life goes on.

        ***   ***   ***

Even if you don't have a popular desire,
don't disclose it to others,
and watchout yourself carefully.
E very body might turn -- like your colour.
And whatever you do may be revealed
on the palms of your hand.
What others like, you do.
In any case return kindness with kindness
and unkindness with unkindness.
A poisonous tree will not yield apricots;
if you want apricots,
go near an apricot tree.
If you desire precious stones,
it is useless to go to the jungles.
If you desire respect from others,
you need to pay more respect to others;

it is difficult for a
proud man to be a great man.
Therefore, it is better to leave pride.
If you are compassionate,
even your enemy will turn friend
Unmeasured roughness may turn
even a son bitter.
Those whose forehead lines run upward,
and whose teeth are white and smile a lot,
such men know human nature well.
Do good deeds and follow the path;
go away with a good reputation, my son.
Those whose forehead lines run down
represent the signs of
poisonous snake's and mad dogs.
They do nothing but bite
day and night;
they follow only bad practice.

        ***   ***   ***

Where good men go, reputation follows.
Such good men bring good results;
and bad results hang
on the neck of mad men.
Bad omens and bad news
follow a bad man.
The yellow Indian pen shaped
these words.
May those be clear on the
white Indian paper of mind.
I have translated Indian into Tibetan,
and Khache Phalu is satisfied.

CHAPTER 8

Moderation

Be humble and patient in all things,
but keep your purpose in mind;
say what pleases others;
use good strategy to achieve your objective.
Then you will achieve your purpose
with sweet mouth.
For such purposes it is better
to be humble.
Many people like the humble.
Many people help such humble folks.
You will enjoy spending your life
drinking tea and chang.[11]
Many will invite you to their homes.
Just as a wild horse is controlled by a bridle,
so you must have self-control.
If you know when to visit,
how long to stay, what to talk,
how to be happy and how to bear suffering,
how much good food to eat
and when to wear good clothes--
then you are the most educated.
Such men are favored by the stars.
But even more important is the future.
Beware your desires don't go beyond limits,
and limits are set by the mind.
Don't live with such mad men.
Don't be led by such bad men.

***   ***   ***

If work knows to limit,
it is ultimately ruined.
If business knows so limits,
it will ultimately be a loss.
If your mouth knows so limits,
 your bottom will get a beating.
If courage knows no limits,
the courageous will finally find himself crying.

   ***   ***   ***

All the sides of life are full
of slopes and precipices;
it is easy to slip and fall down.
Be careful along such a path.
Sounds of life are like nomads playing dice.
No one knows when the right side
of the dice will show.
Keep the losses and gains in mind,
and keep playing the game;
see how you can differentiate
gain from loss.
The path of losses should be blocked.
When you don't know the measure
of loss and gain,
it's better to stay out of the game.
I, Khache Phalu the limitless,
have gone beyond the limit;
precious words have fallen on this paper.
When you estimate the cost,
don't make mistakes.
I have won high stakes, my son.

CHAPTER 9

Food

Don't eat all the good food
or wear all the good clothes;
you might become a slave
to the mouth and the body.
Surely you don't live to eat.
Eyes and stomach can never
be satisfied.
You must know how much to eat.
If your stomach loves
too much food,
you will become fat and lazy.
Rather than having tea and chang
with strings attached,
it is better to eat one's own grass
and drink one's own water.
Rather than having meat from the hunter,[12]
it is better to eat one's own fleas.
Eating and sleeping
only, cows and donkeys do.
Is it good to do such things, my son?

      ***   ***   ***

If dog and stomach get out of hand
there is danger that they might go
after horse and donkey's meat.
If you don't control your stomach,
your good name may be stolen.
If you want a good reputation
hanging all over you,
you better cut the size of your stomach.

The fish loses its life
because it rests too assuredly
in water.
The rat gets trapped
by the throat
because it wants to eat meat.
If the wolf in the wilderness
does not behave itself,
it gets skinned off
because of its hungry nature.
Tigers are feared because
they jump on sheep like a dog.
I have no claim to be an expert,
but I have written black and white.
Even when Khache Phalu is dead,
may his writing last long.

CHAPTER 10

Education

There are two views on one life;
according to one such view
ancestry is important;
father loves his son,
and the son respects his father.
If you think along such lines,
life is not short.
But if not thought so,
the bond between father and son loosens.
If relations worsen,
father and son may become enemies.
Children without parents is inconceivable,
but in fact few have both parents.
If they are alive in the early years,
they are not in the latter years.
Hence, father and son
must keep their love commitment.

      ***   ***   ***

Time waits for no man;
educate your son without loss of time.
The foundation of all education is
learning how to read and write.
It is the king of education.
Education may put
your son on a golden throne.
a classical education may put him
on a tiger-skin seat.
At the monastic college
education is like a mirror.
At the royal court

education is the fruition.
With education you belong
to the expert lineage;
without education you belong
to the unlettered lineage.

       ***   ***   ***

Writing may be as crooked as a bow
but it contains meaning
as straight as an arrow.
The desire for education is universal.
Therefore, those who desire such
education are not scarce,
but men must be truly educated.
Wealth comes and goes;
it may be lost or stolen.
But precious education is an
ever-lasting wealth.
While young, educate your son,
so that you don't have to
educate him when grown up.
Willow can be best straightened while young;
it may breaks when grown old.

       ***   ***   ***

Keeping bad company is like
staying near a poisonous tree;
(it) poisons you.
Bad company is like darkness;
its heart might burn you,
while its cold may give bad effects.

       ***   ***   ***

Think about gain and loss;
talk about both good and bad points.
If you talk about only positive points,
you may be rewarded.

If you talk about only negative points,
you may be punished.
If mother is too quiet,
children may open to bad influence.

      ***   ***   ***

If you polish a stone,
it becomes a precious stone.
If you polish a metal,
it becomes a mirror.
Have an all-rounded education, may son.
If you misbehave,
you might turn my enemy.
These are kindly thoughts;
keep them in mind.

CHAPTER 11

Upbringing

Now listen, those close to the mother's heart;
she is the most affectionate and loving mother.
The child sits before the mother.
If anyone spoils the kid,
it is the mother.
Mother gives her child all kinds of food
and puts on it all kinds of clothes.
The son, spoiled by the mother,
turns out one not even liked by mother.
Many a such son has become a murderer.
Many a such son has become a thief.
If mother does not control her affections,
her children might cause her a nervous
breakdown.
When they steal, beat them up;
when they tell lies, correct them.
If you don't deal with them
when they steal eggs,
soon they will steal hens and horses.
Don't give them too much good food
and good clothes.
Instead teach them good manners.
If not how to do work,
teach them at least how to eat.
A fox's children do not fall
from the ground;
it is a pity if the children of the proud
fall from a precipice.
Beggar's children keep begging;
it is their karma.

When a rich man becomes a beggar,
he becomes a foe.
If you care to listen,
I have told you the implications.
If you care to see,
I have shown the directions.

CHAPTER 12

Gratitute

Now listen, children!
You feel as if you are tigers and leopards
springing out of the forest.
When children come out
of the mother's womb,
they are heavily dependent
on their mother.
Had it not been for their cries "Tser-ter"
they are a piece of meat.
Even if the nipple is
put into their mouths,
yet they cannot walk.
They have ears,
yet they can't understand.
They have two eyes,
yet they can see only the mother.
They have mind,
yet they can think only of the mother.
They don't even know
how to chase the fly from their faces.
They don't even know
how to dust off their eyes.
When they feel cold or hungry,
they disturb their parents' sleep at night.
Where dry the child sleeps
and where wet the parents sleeps
Where comfortable the child sleeps
and where rough the parents use.
While still young,

the children follow their parents' way.
They learn how to do things
such as walking and sitting.
Whatever they can do,
they owe it to their parents.

***   ***   ***

Whatever parents utter,
it is about their son.
They suffer from nervous breakdowns
on account of their son.
They think of and remember
only their son.
Do you now understand
that these two kindly parents grow old?
Do you feel grateful to them?
(If you don't)
you should feel a sense of shame.
Thus you will accumulate good merits.
Above is God,
and below Him are two parents;
there are no more precious beings
than these three beings.
Day and night
listen to parents' advice.
From morning till evening,
serve your parents.
Offer them good food
and see that they like it.
Talk to them about interesting things
and see they appreciate them.
If your parents are satisfied,
then your purpose in this life
and the next is fulfilled.

If parents are not satisfied,
both this and the next are in vain.
Be grateful
when your parents are alive.
Regrets after their passing are useless.
Such regrets last for a long time,
whereas other regrets are felt only once.
Listen, those children with both parents;
keep this precious advice
in the inner recess of your heart.

***   ***   ***

Deceitful tricks or flattery
may spoils the relations between father and son.
If you do this,
you might fall into hell.
Or if you stay near such a man,
your feet might become cold.
You might have heart that
the hill and plain are covered with snow;
and grass with dew drops.

***   ***   ***

No matter from what good lineage
she hails,
woman is an aspect of the devil.
If you listen to whatever she says,
you will be in trouble.
If you let her do what she pleases,
it will cause you, a nervous breakdown.
Beware of the devil and fire.
If you want to be a friend with spirit,
meditate upon a lama.

***   ***   ***

If your clothes are old,
new ones can be tailored.
If you don't have a wife,
a wife can be brought in.
But parents are rare to find.
Your wife cannot replace
the place of your parents.
You should feel ashamed
of yourself with your peers.
Is this what you can do,
despite your boast?
If you don't know the distinction
between your parents and wife
you are worse than a dog.
Even if a dog becomes mad,
it still knows its master.
A man who is worse than a dog
is an egocentric one.
Such a man might turn into an enemy.
An evil man can cause
nervous breakdowns to a hundred.
He misleads others
and is a bad example to the world.
One cow eats another farmer's field;
it blocks the way for all other cows.
Such is the example,
and you should shed your bad habits.
So think carefully, son of a father!
So think straight, brother's heart!
From the place of hope and fear
where you spend summer and winter,
may you go to the place of liberation.
If you have hopes of reward
and fears of punishment,

that is the place to go, my fortunate ones.
When you leave this well-like human existence;
and when you concentrate
upon the essence of death,
you can rely upon God only.
Keep karma in your mind clear
and be ready to go.
Keep the record of good and bad deeds
in mind
and make preparation.
There are many who utter karma
but practitioners of karma
are as scarce as gold.
That is why I regret
from the depth of my heart;
What I have written to-day
is Khache Phalu the madman's talk.
Ignorance has crept into the centre
of my heart.
I don't know myself,
yet I tell others what to do.
I don't see my own fault,
yet I point out other's;
I may have exaggerated
what is cracked.
May the lama forgive me!
May my words be realized
in practice!
May the color and taste harmonize!

      ***   ***   ***

The overflow on to this paper
is precious advice from
the ocean of Khache Phalu's thought.

I have put the nation
in the middle of a well;
it has the beauty of a peacock
and the sweet voice of a garuda.
May happiness spread to all directions!
I have composed these
for the benefit of all.

Footnote to the translator's Introduction

1. A brief account about them may be found in Dawa Norbu, *Red Star Over Tibet* (London: Collins, 1974) p. 88.
2. Rahima Khatoon, Ram Chand Building, Kalimpong, Darjeeling District, West Bengal.
3. Interview with Gulam Rasur on October 25, 1984 in Kalimpong.
4. Dawa Norbu, "Karmic Ethos in Lamaist Society,"A paper delivered to the seminar on 'Religion and Society' at North Bengal University (March 1986)
5. Interview with Rahima Khatoon on October 25, 1984.

Footnotes to the Text

1. Ngo-tsa in this context implies self-restraint arising from a desire for self-respect.
2. Instead of the standard *dKon-mCog gSum*, the author terms it *dKon-mCog rinpoche* thereby adhering to the Islam's monotheism.
3. This line confirms the previous assertion, Godhar being one of the numerous names of Allah.
4. "Only one" again refers to Islamic monothesim.
5. Name of fruit.
6. Being the translation *gTsog-bu*.
7. Denma is the most famous commander of the Tibetan epic hero Gesar of Ling.
8. Believed to be a rare precious stone treasured in Tashi-Lhunpo Monastery, Shigatse.
9. A village near Lhasa, whose donkeys are believed to be always overloaded.
10. In summer metal gets rusted and in winter pottery breaks more easily.
11. Tibetan beer.
12. Another evidence that the author is a Muslim who eats only *halal meat*.